The Rickshaw Chronicles

Tales on Three Wheels from Life as an Edinburgh Rickshaw Driver

Jethro George Gauld

Produced with thanks to the Edinburgh Rickshaw Community and all those who feature in this book.

Dedicated to:

The Shawbusters of Edinburgh.

And:

My mother for giving me the idea for this book.

Disclaimer:

Some of the contents of this book may be unsuitable for those under the age of 15, parental discretion is advised.

Foreword

Rickshaws are a peculiarity of Edinburgh, given its cobbles and steep hills it is not at first a city that you would initially think to suggest plying for trade as a rickshaw driver. Or where it would be the choice mode of transport for thousands of people every year. However the compact nature of the city and winding narrow streets make for an exhilarating experience for customers whether partaking in a slow paced tour of the city's sights or racing from club to club trying to beat their mates to the bar.

Pedicabs first operated in the city of Edinburgh in 2001 with just a few rickshaws and later became a regular feature in the city's streets as popularity grew. At its peak the Edinburgh fleet grew to approximately seventy pedicabs managed by multiple companies and a limited number of independent rider/operators. In 2015 one of the companies sold up and now there are around forty rickshaws in operation in the city. Pedicabs operate at all times of year although outside of the Edinburgh Fringe Festival when all the bikes will be out 24/7, you'll usually only spot around fifteen of them at night on weekends plying for trade.

Working throughout all seasons and meeting people from the whole spectrum of humanity good, bad, interesting and dull, the rickshaw drivers themselves also have a unique perspective upon the city in which they live and work. This book aims to give a unique insight into Edinburgh nightlife, the peculiar world of the rickshaws, regale stories of fares that are particularly memorable or amusing, provide hints for prospective pedicabbers and answer key questions like *"How do you cope with the hills pal?"*

Contents

What it Takes to be a Pedicab Driver and Why Would you Want to be?

"*Eh pal get a real joab!*" (That's not a misspelling rather an accurate phonetic spelling of the way this particular heckle is often pronounced). For many the prospect of working two days per week for most of the year and earning equivalent to five days on a standard wage is what draws them in. Obviously there are the highs and lows; it's not the most reliable of incomes but if you are driven and determined you can make a fair amount.

For many Pedicabbers operating in the city of Edinburgh it allows them to fund themselves through full time study, fund business ideas or community projects or simply top up their income when times are tight. There are also a few for whom it is a longer term option as being essentially self employed suits their lifestyle and it can be more fun than your standard office job.

It is also very important to look after yourself ensuring to stretch properly after every shift as demonstrated by the Simpson brothers. The physical toll of the job on riders means that those who don't look after themselves risk injury.

It takes more than legs of steel to survive off the backs of these three wheeled horses. You need to be strong of both body and mind to get through a shift. For example the top ten heckles are listed below:

1. *"PEDAL FAAAAASSSSSTTTTTEEEEEERRRR!"* (Often from a man eating chips)
2. *"Take me to Glasgow!"*
3. *"Do a wheelie!"*
4. *"Ey Rick, Rick Shaw!"*
5. *"Come on wid' ya horse!"* (Commonly from Irish Customers)
6. Hen parties will typically shout *"Nice Bum!"* then go for a cheeky pinch with male riders.
7. *"Come on Wiggins!"*
8. Clapping/Cheering of some description
9. *"Can I Have a Go?!"*
10. *"I could run faster!"* (As you struggle up a steep incline)

Top Responses to this include:

1. Blunt indifference
2. *"Aye hop in, £2000 plus expenses to Glasgow"*
3. *"If this hill were steeper we already would be"*
4. Again, blunt indifference
5. Encourage them to sing a song from the homeland
6. *"Pound a Pinch ladies"*
7. *"I'm better than wiggins!"*
8. Start singing a motivational theme such as *"I need a hero"* until passersby/passengers join in. Usually works a treat.
9. *"I'd love to but health and safety forbids me"*
10. *"Yes, you could run faster but not for 8 hours"*

The Average Pedicabber

Your average pedicabber (see the stats on the following couple of pages) is young, highly educated and driven by a desire to improve their lot.

What is interesting to note is that many rickshaw drivers started the job as some kind of stop gap, one driver replied that his initial plan was to do the job for *"Long enough to earn back the 2.5k I spent in fresher's week"*; others start as a way of building themselves a more stable foundation *"I started because I wanted some stability in my life and to make new friends as well as get fit and earn some money."* and others wanted to be their own boss for a change *"I'd had enough of minimum wage bar jobs, trapped in a sweaty nightclub with a venomous boss who never let anyone request time off. I quit one night and was skint for a month before a friend from university told me about rickshawing, and gave me some guy's number; turned out to be more life changing than I could ever have imagined"*. For most it is addictive, the thrill of not knowing what each night will bring and the buzz that comes with a successful night keeps many drivers on the 'shaws for several years.

Unsurprisingly this lot are probably in the top 5% in Scotland in terms of cardiovascular fitness with more than a few riders using the job as a way to train for professional cycle races. This desire to be active is reflected in the top hobbies listed by the 38 pedicabbers who responded to a survey for this book. Cycling, Skiing, Orienteering, Judo, Running, Football, Rugby, Cricket and Sailing all feature however this is mirrored by the need to relax after such physical exertion listing activities such as gardening, cooking, sleeping, DIY, music, writing and brewing craft beer as their other top hobby.

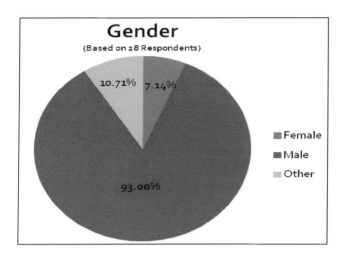

Gender
(Based on 28 Respondents)

10.71% 7.14%

93.00%

■ Female
■ Male
■ Other

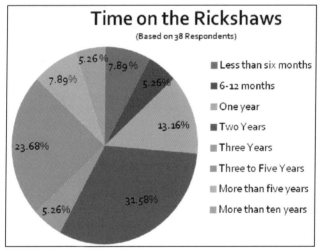

Time on the Rickshaws
(Based on 38 Respondents)

5.26% 7.89%
7.89% 5.26%
23.68% 13.16%
5.26% 31.58%

■ Less than six months
■ 6-12 months
■ One year
■ Two Years
■ Three Years
■ Three to Five Years
■ More than five years
■ More than ten years

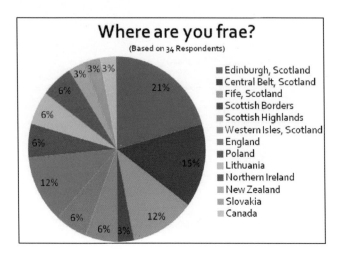

Where are you frae?

(Based on 34 Respondents)

- Edinburgh, Scotland
- Central Belt, Scotland
- Fife, Scotland
- Scottish Borders
- Scottish Highlands
- Western Isles, Scotland
- England
- Poland
- Lithuania
- Northern Ireland
- New Zealand
- Slovakia
- Canada

21%, 15%, 12%, 3%, 6%, 6%, 12%, 6%, 6%, 3%, 3%, 3%, 6%

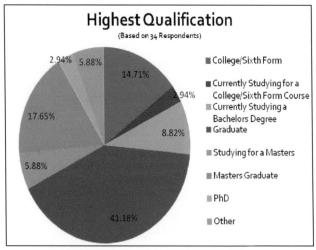

Highest Qualification

(Based on 34 Respondents)

- College/Sixth Form
- Currently Studying for a College/Sixth Form Course
- Currently Studying a Bachelors Degree
- Graduate
- Studying for a Masters
- Masters Graduate
- PhD
- Other

14.71%, 2.94%, 8.82%, 41.18%, 5.88%, 17.65%, 5.88%, 2.94%

The Geeky Bit: Rickshaw Specifications - How do we Manage Those Hills?

The answer: brute force essentially. All the rickshaws in Edinburgh are made by a Bath Based company called Cycles Maximus; these steel framed beasts are pretty hefty at 70-90kg depending on the type of cab you have on them. This weight means that they are built to last but despite some pretty nifty gearing they are still essentially designed with flat cities like Amsterdam in mind rather than say the steep cobbles of Victoria Street. That said they do perform pretty well (at £4000 a pop you'd hope so), their compact size (2m long by 1.1m wide) means they can fit through the tightest of gaps. With a 27 speed drive train composed of a 9 speed sprocket connected to a 3 speed SRAM hub makes climbing those hills possible and delivering power to the wheels via a split differential allowing the wheels to turn independently meaning these things can turn on a dime. Combine this with high end brakes off a quad bike, a cab and a blanket and you've got one nifty passenger vehicle with zero emissions and door to door service.

Why no electric assist? I hear you ask. The answer: us riders may go all night but the batteries can't hack it. Also the council don't like electric assist vehicles and honestly we couldn't charge as much per fare if they we had any form of mechanical assistance up those hills. Part of the fun for some people is seeing you sweat; you often don't know the customer's background so if they are in a low standing job then what is wrong with them enjoying having someone else do all the hard work for once?

Shifters for hub and cassette gears (27 in total)

32 tooth front chain ring

9 speed 11-34 tooth cassette

3 speed hub with internal gears

Hydraulic disc brakes for rapid deceleration

22 tooth rear sprocket driving a split differential allowing the wheels to turn at different speeds when turning

Places of Trade

The Classy Part of Town

The New town of Edinburgh consists of a grid pattern of streets constructed 300 years ago to honour the union of England and Scotland. Five major streets run parallel to each other, Princes Street, Rose Street named after the English rose, George Street after king George IV, Thistle Street after the Scottish emblem and Queen Street. With its mix of high end bars, popular tourist spots and traditional pubs on Rose Street, new town nightlife appears to attract a strange mix of clientele.

This clientele typically includes the very wealthy, the wannabe wealthy spending money they don't have, hen parties and the occasional lost stag do wandering the streets confused as to why none of the upmarket bars on George Street will let in 16 beer swilling lads 'fresh' from the rose street challenge (discussed in a later chapter). In the New Town a pedicabber can typically expect to gather a great deal of custom from women in outrageously high heels seeking the Cheryl Cole look, lads approaching hypothermia because they are wearing only a t-shirt when it's -10 and the aforementioned stag party wanting to escape to a less discerning part of town.

It is also where you can expect to find a lot of business after 3am when the clubs close and you will typically see several pedicabs waiting outside some of the busier clubs around this time.

In the Shadow of History

Nightlife in the old town of Edinburgh is a rather more mixed affair; the Grassmarket and the Cowgate sit in a valley below the castle funnelling folk down toward the many pubs and more budget friendly clubs the city has to offer. In rickshaw terms it is something of a honey pot from where you can expect to earn a significant proportion of your business ferrying folk along the Cowgate or giving lifts to Edinburgh's West end.

The Cowgate

The Cowgate was once the domain of wealthy traders until the construction of the bridges in the 18th and 19th century (North Bridge in 1772 (Later rebuilt in the 1890's), South Bridge in 1788, George IV Bridge in 1832). Once completed these bridges formed the new street level and the surrounding tenement blocks and other buildings grew up to their level sometimes exceeding 14 floors. Those who could afford it moved to the upper floors while the lower levels and hidden vaults became the domain of miscreants and undesirables.

In some ways not much has changed. In modern times the Cowgate has become a focal point for Edinburgh's nightlife featuring multiple dance venues of varying reputation. Aside from potential punters wandering the streets, after 10pm pedicabs have the Cowgate pretty much to themselves as engine powered vehicles are officially not permitted. Being able to take this direct route between venues is a key selling point for customers wishing to travel from A to B as fast as possible.

The Grassmarket

Once the site of public executions; the Grassmarket now offers other sources of public entertainment. It is populated by 10 pubs of varying capacity and reputation with several others within close proximity, some of these pubs are the only ones in the city likely to allow in large stag parties. It is also a favourite among students of Edinburgh's four universities and the best place in the city to see groups in fancy dress.

Mind your head though; a local by law still exists whereby provided the phrase *"GARDYLOO!"* is shouted as a warning, residents are perfectly within their rights to discard whatever form of waste water or other effluent from their window that they wish to dispose of.

Flesh for Sale

Almost adjacent to the Grassmarket is an area known colloquially as "*The Pubic Triangle*", at the junction on the corner of Bread Street, East Fountainbridge and Lauriston Street sit three strip clubs forming the corners of this unholy trinity.

One of the venues is named the Burke and Hare. The name gives a nod to the infamous trade in body parts which used to thrive in the city and that in some senses the business of strip clubs is still very much a trade in human flesh. Indeed the moral debate around this trade is as alive as ever. The venues lure in punters with the promise of £5 dances and cut price drinks. When asked about the experience lads typically either reply with great enthusiasm *"Aye it's great, fanny in yer face fer a fiver!"* or with a hint of embarrassment *"Oh, I only went cos all me mates went. Not too fussed by this sort of thing meself"*.

Around the triangle a number of other strip clubs and other venues such as 'saunas' and swingers clubs have sprung up. It's an example of how Edinburgh is very much a Jeckle and Hyde City. In the day you'd probably walk straight past these places unaware of their existence. Meanwhile at night while the other shops close their shutters the neon lights fire up luring in drunken lads and a surprising number of ladies like a moth to a flame. Although the main trade is stag groups, the triangle also appears to have become a rite of passage for some fresher's from one of the four universities in the city. It's quite common in the first few weeks of term to witness mixed groups of first year students wandering in seemingly unaware of what's inside.

The Bridges

This refers to the area around north and south bridge. Other than the ridge on which the royal mile is constructed between the castle and Holyrood Palace this vast area of the city centre is almost completely artificial as in the late 1800's all the surrounding buildings were built up to the new street level create by the North and South Bridges linking the New Town to the Old Town and further south toward Newington.

For the Pedicabber this is where you might try your luck during the fringe or at 4am when you might glean a final lift from those visiting the only pizza place open after the clubs close. Quite often though it turns into a good chance to have a chat, compare earnings and exchange stories from the night that has just been before heading home to hit the hay.

The Royal Mile

The Royal Mile is probably one of the most famous roads in the UK. It consists of the Canongate, Highstreet and Lawnmarket and measuring almost exactly one mile from the castle to the doors of Holyrood Palace. The buildings here are some of the oldest in Edinburgh and the many closes which wind their way to and from the mile each have a few tales to tell including some grisly secrets best forgotten to the winds of time. From the perspective of the pedicabber this tourist hotspot generally offers fairly slim pickings in terms of fares aside from during the annual Fringe Festival.

Creatures of the Night

Animalis inebriatum: The Road Walker

Often seen walking down the middle of the road in the face of oncoming traffic as after a few drinks the pavement becomes too narrow a path to follow.

***Homo infuriata*: Anger embodied**

Most likely to be seen in cuffs by the end of the night, unfortunately some people associate a good night out with looking for a fight.

Homo ululates: The Howler

Often seen during a full moon howling or singing, one pedicabber once witnessed a man howling to the moon in Hunter's Square for 45 minutes.

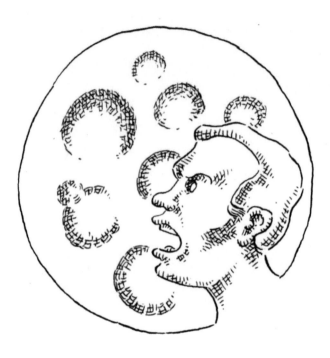

Sedentes frigus: The Stair Guardians

If you venture onto George Street between 3am and 4am on a Saturday or a Sunday you are likely to see groups of smartly dressed but very cold looking people huddling together on the steps of the many businesses and shops in denial about how long it may take them to find a taxi.

Amicus stultorum: The Hugger

Probably the nicest type of drunk you will meet as you wander through the streets of Edinburgh on a Friday or Saturday night. Typically they just want to compliment you, shake your hand and bid you good night.

Customers and Lost Causes

This section aims to give an insight into the kinds of potential customers a rickshaw driver is likely to encounter during an average night.

The Spoil Sport

The most frustrating thing as a pedicab driver is when a massive group are all keen to go somewhere but one of their friends railroads the negotiations because they don't want to spend this or they don't want to go where the birthday boy, bride to be or stag suggest. This person is most likely to be found abandoned and lost in the small hours of the morning.

"Evening lads, where are you looking to go?"

"Awesome! Rickshaws! Let's do it boys" the lads pile into the two waiting bikes except for one who pipes up

"Nah, I'll walk. I'd rather save my money for beer." Crossing his arms in an act of defiance.

"But it's Steve's stag, he wants to go to the next bar and these guys are gonna take us. Come on Mike it'll be fun"

"I'll catch up"

"But you won't know where to go"

"Hop in Mike, we'll get you there!" Try the drivers in a final attempt but he walks off.

"Sorry lads" says the best man to the riders *"We can't leave a man behind though if he carries on like this we might have to..."*

Difficult Customers

Mix alcohol with a short temper and unfortunately some customers can be abusive, especially when they hear the price. Often the best way to either get these folk in the bike or get rid of them is to fight fire with fire; they may well simply be testing you to see if you flinch on your price. A story of three middle aged ladies who stumbled out of the Beehive into my rickshaw springs to mind.

"Eh, how much te city nightclub?"

"Alright ladies yeah I'll get you to city, is it the three of you?"

"Aye but how much?"

"It's quite far but I'll give you a fair deal, I'll take you there for about £6 each you happy with that?"

"Fuckin' naw; each?! Ahm a single mother!" (Here we go, he thought to himself)

"Yes ladies, it's hard work hence the price but I'll make it good fun"

"Not each I'll give you a tenner and that's that."

"I think 6 each is a fair price if you're not happy go try your luck elsewhere"

"Naw your fuckin' takin' us an' you'll get a tenner fer it!"

"Look I've been polite up until now but I've got a fucking masters degree! I know what my time is worth. Either get in the bike or get away it's your choice!"

Miraculously with that they were in, were quite chatty and at the end of the fare they even gave a tip. Funny how some people work.....

Headless Hens

From observation the success of a hen or bachelor party is correlated either with the presence of a plan for the night or by the presence of some form of leadership of the group; one voice, usually the best man or maid of honour to act as the final word in what the group does (unless of course your whole party has attended a workshop about consensus decision making).

Not only does this make the night a better flow and avoid potential conflict it also makes the life of the pedicab driver much, much, easier as all you have to do is ask one person where to go and the rest will follow. There is nothing more confusing than a crowd of 20 or so slightly tipsy shrill voiced women clucking different place names at you and at each other when you are trying to decipher their destination. This is often accompanied by the mother of the bride trying her best to embarrass her daughter by flirting with one of the drivers, sometimes specifying which one they want to go with *"Ooh your nice, I want your rickshaw!"* or in some cases, trying to match the driver up the bride's sister.

Lost Souls and Wandering Stags

You meet a lot of lost souls while working on the rickshaws. Some folk are lost in the metaphysical sense where they just need to chat to someone for a couple of minutes to settle their soul. Others are lost in the sense that they need directions and some are just a little worse for wear after a few too many beverages. Expectant grooms often seem to fall into all three of these categories.

With some stag parties simply embarrassing the groom is not sufficient; indeed the aim of the night is to get the 'lucky fella' as lost as possible. At some point in the night after a sufficient amount of alcohol, lacking power on his phone or details of the accommodation the stag will be spun around and sent on an errand in the opposite direction to his hotel while his mates scarper. There appears to be a seasonal ebb and flow to this phenomenon as for some reason this situation occurs more frequently on some nights than others.

Deciphering where these wandering stags might wish to reside is quite a feat of linguistic achievement as often they are beyond the point of stringing together a sentence. "*You alright Sir? You look a bit lost?*" The stag awakes from his snooze against the phone box. "*Jaaaryy, bhin*" as he attempts but fails to formulate a sentence, further prompting is required with this one. "*Where you trying to get to?*" I start off the usual destinations for stag parties "*Chippy, Pub, Strippers..?*" "*bah, noonnnnn*" he replies, drunk speak for no. Wishing to help the man and hopefully get a fare I persevere, "*Nightclub, Hostel, Hotel?*" "*Gaaaah!*" he gargles attempting to raise his finger to signal yes, I think we're onto a winner but still need to narrow it down. "*Ok Hotel, which one? Travelodge, Premier Inn, Holiday Inn, Jury's Inn*", "*Gaah*" comes the excited reply sensing he may not have to spend the night sleeping in a urine scented phone box using his kebab as a pillow.

I double check: "*Ok so Jury's Inn?*"He grunts, nods and collapses gratefully into the rickshaw where he immediately covers himself with the blanket and remains under it for the entire trip home. He will have no memory of how he got home, but the important thing is that he did get home which he wouldn't have managed without the help of a rickshaw.

Directions, taxi queues and know it alls

People can sometimes be so certain of themselves that even though part of their self conscious realises they are lost and that they should ask for directions. Most pedicab drivers are happy to help such folk with directions or give out advice, partly as this can often be a good way to attract business. The shrewd pedicabbers will also know where in town people are best getting a cab from to head further out and will happily oblige with directions or transporting customers to these locations. However it is a tad frustrating when the person then walks the opposite way to the direction you just told them or when someone going far out of town ignores your advice that standing on a deserted pedestrian street waving their arm around at 5am won't get them a taxi any time in the near future.

The Sheikh and His Friends

This was one of the most original bachelor parties and it was clear they really respected their friend as a lot of effort had gone into the outfits including working radio earpieces:

Stag Security Agent 1: "*Bravo, Bravo Two Zero over!*"

Agent 2: "*The Sheikh is in transit, the Sheikh is in transit over!*"

Agent 3: "*Clear the Way, VIP Coming through!*"

Agent 4: "*Jim, Jim do you read over!*"

Agent 5: "*Reading loud and clear!*"

Agent 4: "*We need that road clear stat!*"

Five of the stag do run ahead of the rickshaw stopping traffic and clearing a path through the crowds on the Cowgate. Meanwhile the other Eight or so lads run alongside the rickshaw forming a protective ring for the stag "*The Sheikh*" helping pull the bike along whenever an uphill was reached.

The Irish

Rickshaw drivers love the Irish and fortunately the Irish seem to love rickshaws.

Your typical Irish stag do drinks from 9am in the morning until the clubs close at 3am at which point they can be identified from a distance by the alarm call: *"Where's the drink, ere where's the drink!?"*. They'll also do anything *"for the banter"* or *"Craic"* (Pronounced Crack); this could include getting in a pedicab, going to the casino, embarking on a midnight tour of the city's finest establishments or a combination of the three.

Although they can be rowdy and drive a hard bargain at first, Irish customers are among the most entertaining and most eager to tip of any clientele a pedicabber is likely to encounter. Provided you don't mind being called *"horse"* of course.

The Valleys

During the Six Nations or other rugby internationals, whenever Wales play Scotland at Murrayfield you know you are in for a busy night. Edinburgh is temporarily annexed by Cardiff and the town turns red with welsh flags, dragons and people in fancy dress.

Welsh passengers have a habit of referring to you as "drive", as in "'ere drive where's good to go?" Out for a good time riders have told stories of the welsh taking their trophies from the night on the rickshaw with them ranging from traffic comes to bikes.

On one lift, the remaining three members of a welsh stag do insisted on bringing a bicycle that they'd found with them. During the journey they rang all their mates announcing they were getting a bike to take them with their bike back to their hotel, the hotel was at the airport so the driver in question was tasked with hailing them a taxi from Haymarket station; the taxi driver seemed a tad unimpressed with the bike being piled into his cab by two stocky welsh lads.

Weddings

Although not something you will encounter every shift, weddings are probably the most enjoyable fares you will ever encounter as a rickshaw driver. Your passengers will almost always be really happy, not in any particular hurry to be anywhere and you know you'll be making a decent amount of money for the fare. This means that as the driver you can relax as well, take the time to talk to them and also pick a more enjoyable scenic route through the city rather than simply getting from A to B as quickly as possible. This is after all their special day. What can be stressful is when someone is late to pick up the rickshaw before heading to meet the wedding party or when they turn up looking really scruffy and you need to send them home to change into something that doesn't have grease stains all over it.

Mixed Morals

Last Night of Freedom

People seem to interpret this common phrase very differently on their stag or hen do especially when there is so much temptation on the streets.

One fare sticks in the memory as three Irish Lads piled in the rickshaw with one simple request from the best man: "*Take us to the titties! This man needs some titties!*" to which the groom to be replied "*I'm not sure about this, I'm getting married next week*" we set off anyway as the best man pushed a £20 note into my hand.

The debate between them continued as we sped down king stables road but seemed to conclude with the best man exclaiming to his pal "Ah *te fuck wid ya, you're goin' to the place and that's that*". Meanwhile the third guy seemed happy to go along with whatever but piped up "*I need a bank machine!*". While waiting at the bank machine the groom to be didn't seem happy with the situation and said: "*I can't do this, the t'ing is I've only got the eyes for one girl, I won't go to the strippers*".

I was pleasantly surprised by his apparent moral conviction, as too was the best man who took a few seconds to recover from the shock before replying: "*Ah fine, but you'll go te the whores won't ya!*" to which the groom to be replied "*Well only if we share one I suppose*".

At this moment the third bloke returned, having just heard the final decision he announced: "*Whores is it?! I better get more cash!*"

Pedicab Swag

Before, during and after a shift you often come across discarded items of interest and/or value that have been discarded by other residents and revellers of Edinburgh during the course of the night.

Unless it is something like a wallet or phone where you would try to reunite it with the owner this booty can be a welcome bonus to your earnings over the course of a night or simply useful to play a prank on one of your fellow riders by decorating their bike.

Common items include umbrellas, fancy dress outfits, giant inflatables (sheep, phallic symbols etc...), miscellaneous clothing, money, jackets but sometimes you come across some really useful stuff like furniture sets, camera and speaker tripods, street sweeper's brooms, unopened bottles of whisky and bikes that have been abandoned.

Unsure of Their Actions

It had been a strange night with a lot of agro on the streets. While cycling up the Cowgate two young lads jumped in, they were quite smartly dressed but clearly in a hurry and gave me £20 upfront to get to Lothian Road. I wasn't in a mood to barter for more. As we whizzed down the Grassmarket they started to explain what had just happened to them.

"See we were just leaving the club and saw this overweight arsehole picking on some deaf cu#t (In Scotland cu#t is not necessarily and insult and can merely refer to someone you don't know) *and couldn't believe no one was stopping this or that the police weren't helping"* says one. The other lad goes on to say *"We're both in the army so we know how to defend ourselves"*. *"Aye right"* pipes up the first lad *"We weren't sure what to do at first but stepped in as the deaf guy had no clue what was going on, anyway the big guy swung for me so I gave him the ol' left hook. I wasn't expecting him to keel over after one blow mind. It was like a giant blubbery tree falling to the ground in slow motion. Funny and he had it coming but I didn't mean to hurt him that much. I was just trying to defend someone who couldn't defend themselves!".* The second lad pipes up again *"And that's when we saw you! So we scarpered before the polis* (Police) *arrived."*

The discussion went on throughout the journey with me trying to find out more details before helping them decide whether they had stepped over the line. By the time I dropped them off the matter of whether, in their opinion, they had done the right thing in stepping in to stop what they saw as an injustice remained unresolved and they were still discussing it as they disappeared into the neon glow of the next club.

Riders and Rules

Pedicab Pseudonyms

Many of the rickshaw riders have a gimmick to help attract custom. This ranges from kilts to rugby tops and full blown fancy dress. One particular rider consistently wore a Mr Messy shirt; he noticed that customers would rarely ask his real name rather calling him Mr Messy instead. Other characters are Superscot, Anchorman and several editions of 'I wanna be rapha/hoy/wiggins'. Old timer pedicabbers often comment how lycra is a relatively recent trend. Around certain times of year you may also find Santa Clause, Elves, witches, where's Wally and William Wallace.

The Mechanic

Occasionally something breaks on one of the rickshaws. Most of the Pedicab companies operate with a roving mechanic; this is usually one of the regular riders who assists other riders with breakdowns in exchange for reduced rent to hire the pedicab.

He or she will happily help with everything except for punctures which are the responsibility of the individual rider to sort out. It is wise to be nice to whoever is on duty as mechanic as they are also busy trying to attract custom and it can be frustrating to cycle across town to fix something the rider probably could have done themselves.

Key words for ensuring a slower response time for your breakdown include: "*Hurry up, it's busy!*", "*I've got a puncture can you come show me how to fix it?*", "*I'm in the arse end of nowhere with a snapped chain and need you to hurry*". However if you are polite to the mechanic they will usually come promptly and do their utmost to fix things. Even so there are the occasional breakdowns which cannot be repaired in the street meaning the rider has to push their pedicab back to the depot and swap bikes. While waiting for the mechanic you will also receive many offers of help from folk claiming to be engineers "*an tha' eh..*" which usually proceeds as follows:

"*Eh Pal, You crashed or summit?*" asks mr know it all, "*Er, no just fixing the chain for my mate here.*" Gesturing with a head nod toward the other pedicab driver. "*Ah reet, ah see. You need help? I fix bikes all the time like?*" Goes to move the bike...... Alarmed grunts resonate from under the cab. "No thanks! And careful you nearly pulled the bike over on me there." "Oh Sorry pal, I was just trying to help" genuinely offended that help is not wanted from someone who's had a few too many bevvies to be of use "I'm fine cheers.... hope you have a good night." The highly qualified mechanical consultant staggers off into the night while the issue is soon sorted and the Mechanic cycles off into the night to fix the next breakdown.

Obey the Rules!

Edinburgh pedicabs are probably some of the most strictly regulated in the country with each rider having to complete a training session, agree to follow the rules of the road and be approved for a street trader's license before they can hit the streets plying for business in the city centre.

This is self policed with any rider caught breaking the Highway Code for example facing a suspension. The council and police also appear to spend a rather disproportionate amount of time telling pedicabs where to park, often resulting in them not noticing the car that just sped down a closed road endangering pedestrians.

There is also a set of unwritten rules among Edinburgh pedicab drivers, if you choose not to follow these rules you will find it hard to make friends. These rules include not jumping the queuing system when in a rank, not undercutting other riders or at least waiting until after the person has walked away from the negotiations, splitting tips on group lifts and on nights when the weather turns nasty there is an unspoken obligation to cheer up your other riders with food, hugs, tea or jokes.

Ranking up or Raking it in.

Most Pedicabbers will agree that to do well you have to be motivated to speak to people and take a positive approach to speaking to potential Customers; often peoples don't realise they 'need' a rickshaw ride until you've mentioned the best club in town to them. Indeed this can be the most entertaining part of the job as you meet all sorts of characters.

Sometimes in doing so you meet people who may be able to help you further your daytime career or in the case of one or two pedicabbers find that special someone. However on some nights there is a great temptation to succumb to sitting in ranks with your fellow riders. Serious matters are often discussed while in ranks and impassioned debate about political events or tactics in cycle racing can go on for a while. Usually, however, discussion revolves around the best and worst fares of the night so far.

Many riders consider sitting in ranks to be giving up on their night, as in doing so you limit the number of potential customers you encounter. From personal observation, riders who make a habit of sitting in the fateful Biddy's or George street ranks typically earn about half as much as those who are constantly roving the streets approaching potential passengers.

Our Spinach

In Edinburgh there is a sense of comradeship among pedicabbers with a strict set of unwritten rules and willingness to help each other out. At first however, it is quite a bit to take in. The first night is hard whether it's your first ever night or you've been away from the bikes for a long time. You've likely not brought enough food and have been taking fares so cheap that other riders wouldn't touch them with a 10 metre pole. As such by 2am those who are either new or back on the bikes after a long stint away can be spotted by how exhausted they look. At this moment there is nothing better than another pedicabber chucking a can of Nurishment_TM in your direction like a golden glow of energy rich goodness. Nurishment is an enriched drink made from condensed milk locally known as junkie juice, this is our version of popeye's spinach. It tastes disgusting (like metallic gloop) but if you can get past the feeling of nausea experienced immediately after consumption, it will help see you through to the end of the night.

Good Deeds

Street Pastors

Of an evening in Edinburgh, in amongst the revellers and likely lads you might just spot the Edinburgh Street Pastors. These volunteers are seen on the streets every weekend helping anyone who needs it. Sometimes this is simply chatting to someone while they wait for their lift though they also make a point of checking up on homeless people and helping lost people find their way home. They are also locally famous for their free flip flops given to ladies who just can't bear their high heels any longer.

For more information visit: http://edinburgh.streetpastors.org.uk/

Christian Coffee

Need a coffee? Fancy a chat about morality and spirituality? These are just the folks to see. Every Friday and Saturday night these guys offer free hot drinks on Rose Street and the Cowgate for absolutely free. Some of the volunteers will try to convince you to turn up to church on Sunday but they are by no means pushy and provide a valuable service. Also on the streets are the Bethany Christian Trust who sponsor a meals van providing vital meals and hot drinks to homeless people or anyone else in need (sometimes this includes pedicabbers if you ask nicely for a cuppa).

The Music Makers

A delightful diversity of Musicians ply for fame and fortune or simply play for fun on the streets of Edinburgh. These include the usual guitar wielding singers playing classic brit pop tunes along with those who choose fare more niche instruments. Being Scotland the bagpipe is most commonly employed on the Royal mile or Princes Street filling the air with songs of the nation. In the new town along Rose Street and George Street can be heard the music of Pink Floyd and Oasis tribute artists.

In the Old town on the Cowgate you will often find a very talented drummer playing on a drum kit made of recycled barrels or sometimes a guitar player called Jamie who plays for fun rather than purely for money.

Special Missions and Feats of Daring Do

For some folk, a night out on the "toon" is not complete without "improving" the city in some way or completing some sort of challenge in the name of banter. For example, the folk of Glasgow like to honour the Duke of Wellington statue by decorating him with a traffic cone atop his head. Edinburgh meanwhile has a number of statues of philosophers such as John David Hume which are regularly decorated with a suitably white and orange crown. There are also a few occasions each night where Pedicabbers play a key role in these sporting activities in the name of 'banter'. This chapter is meant to provide a small sample of these extraordinary acts of physical, gastronomical and mental exertion.

The Rose Street Challenge

Rose Street is approximately one mile long consisting of a mix of cafes, small shops and bars. 14 of the pubs on Rose Street are included in the rose street challenge to make it from one end of Rose Street to the other having a pint in every pub along the way.

At time of publication these pubs included:

1. Scott's Bar
2. Dirty Dick's
3. The Rose and Crown
4. The Shoogly Peg
5. The Black Cat
6. The Amber Rose
7. The Kenilworth
8. The Shack
9. Element
10. The Auld Hundred
11. The Rose Street Brewery
12. The Black Rose
13. Milnes Bar
14. The Abbotsford

While not exactly athletic, it's beginnings lay with some of Scotland's finest athletes. Originally an endeavour of Rugby and Cricket clubs the challenge is now popular among visitors to the city. Completing the Rose street challenge is a feat of binge drinking prowess which will award you a combination of respect from your friends and a thumping hangover the next day. It requires not only an iron stomach but a wallet to match it given that the average Rose Street pub will charge you upwards of £4.50 for a pint. It is also wise to do this in small groups as pedicabbers get a lot of business from transporting large groups of lads to the friendlier pastures of the Grassmarket after they've spent hours being rejected from bars in the new town.

In Search of Food

This is a remarkably common request; folk leave the pubs and clubs and want food. Unfortunately, a quirk of Edinburgh is that very few takeaways can afford to fork out the fee for the late licence to be open beyond 3am which it so happens coincides with when most pubs and clubs are open until. As such customers rely on your local knowledge of the 'best' joints in town to get a pie, a pizza or a samosa in the early hours of the morning. Usually this is en-route home or after 3am when most takeaways are shut pedicabs can whisk people along to exotic venues such as the Pie Shop or Pizza Paradise for a small fee. Sometimes customers just want to have a bit of fun and get the VIP treatment. The challenge is to get them their before their mates so they get to order first and get away in a flash holding their bounty aloft like a trophy before scoffing the lot on the return journey.

Race to the Strippers

For many stag parties having the stag utterly embarrassed and degraded in some of Edinburgh's sleazier establishments is a highlight of their weekend. However being unfamiliar with the city they often call upon the services of rickshaws to get them there in good time.

Sometimes the group may be unwilling to pay the going rate however adding in a bit of competition can help swing the deal in your favour, particularly if you get the best man on board with your suggestion. The mere mention of a race will typically have the group piling into rickshaws and arguing over which rider is going to be the fastest. The answer to that is whichever rider is promised the biggest tip will be the fastest. All other things being equal it will be the rider who wasn't out drinking the previous night. The best races are where the riders are fairly evenly matched allowing for some good banter between bikes throughout the journey.

The Dragon flies to North Berwick

Although there is now a zone which riders obey records do exist for the longest lift, the biggest fare and the most earned in one night. Often such fares are achieved on a rider's final ever shift as they wish to go out with a bang and are less concerned about retaining their licence. The current distance record is Edinburgh to North Berwick (22.5 miles) with the round trip completed in 7 hours on the final night of the Edinburgh Fringe Festival with two passengers.

Uma Draggon, the rider in question, had flipped a coin for the lift after the two gents had approached separate riders. They had been trying to get a taxi and didn't want to wait until 10am to for the next train so figured it would be funny to get a rickshaw home and break some sort of record in the process. Apparently once they got to Portobello and Uma realised they were serious about going all the way, the two guys just curled up and went to sleep under the duvet. They woke up just in time to see sunrise over Aberlady Bay.

Upon completion of the journey Uma had her photograph taken with her two customers who along with paying the rather large fare also bought her breakfast before her return journey.

Uma later said that although tiring, the lift was really enjoyable and something she says she'll always remember "I guess I'll be able to boast to my grandkids about this!" She also hopes that it's a record that never gets beaten.

Approximate route (contains Stamen Toner/OSM data)

Conquering the Impossible

There are a number of hills within the city centre of Edinburgh that the majority of the population wouldn't even attempt on their own bike let alone a rickshaw. Within the rickshaw community though these are seen as challenges to be conquered and great pride is taken in beating these fierce adversaries, partly as fares involving some of these routes occur very rarely so a rider may have to wait a number of years before an opportunity arises to put his or her endurance to the test (some of the old team would also add Arthur's seat but that's out of the zone these days...). Others on this list are regular routes that must be overcome on a regular basis, sometimes several times per night. It is not simply a matter of stamina but also of the ability to keep customers entertained on such journeys where the pace can be rather slow. Failure can result in humiliation and lost income but success can bring significant rewards for those willing to have a go.

1. The Royal Mile (From the Parliament to Lawnmarket) (Gain of 120m over 0.8 miles)

    This only really occurs during the Edinburgh Festival and can catch riders out with their pricing as the mile is usually uphill of everywhere else in the city but sometimes tourists will request a lift from the bottom to the top near the bridges or the castle. This equates to almost a mile of constant uphill over cobbles with other road users often causing you to stop and start.

2. Market Street from Waverley Bridge (Gain of 50m over 0.2 miles)

This hill is particularly steep; most pedicabbers never attempt it and elect to go up North Bridge or via the Royal Mile if they take a lift from Waverley up to High Street or Near the Castle. For those who manage it, they can be safe knowing that they have earned every single penny of the fare they asked for.

3. The Mound (Gain of 80m over 0.3 miles)

Although the most direct route from New town to George IV Bridge, this hill presents a mighty challenge that many new riders choose to avoid. The steepest section is approximately halfway up and is also on a camber forcing you to either pedal at an angle or stay in the saddle which can be a struggle with three hefty blokes in the back. It is usually at this section where you will also need to keep your customers entertained when they realise that you are travelling much slower than walking pace but once past this nasty corner you can be assured that the worst is behind you. This is also the point at which to get your customers singing "We Are the Champions My Friends!" as you spin your way over the top of the Mound onto the Royal Mile in a blaze of glory.

4. Johnston Terrace from Lothian Road (Gain of 90m over 0.6 miles)

"Take us to the Castle pal" From the west end the most direct route to the castle or top of the Royal Mile is via Johnston Terrace, other routes either involve the Mound or losing altitude only to have to climb both the Grassmarket and Victoria Street. This hill is also made famous by the short film 'Three Legged Horses' which follows an Edinburgh Rickshaw driver through the course of his last shift. In terms of altitude gain this is a bit higher than the mound however the smooth road surface and fairly constant gradient mean you can get into a rhythm and power through. The key to completing this fare is being able to either get your customers singing or keeping the banter up along the way. Lads out on a stag love a bit of bravado and once at the top it's a brilliant opportunity to do a victory lap around St Giles Cathedral.

These guys sang the rocky theme all the way up Johnston Terrace.

5. Blackfriars Street (Gain of 50m over 0.1 miles)
    Although short this long straight street with cobbles and
    constant steep gradient is probably one of the toughest routes
    from the Cowgate up to the Bridges area of the Royal Mile. It is
    also a tough psychological battle as you can see the top and it
    never seems to get much closer with each pedal stroke.

6. Victoria Street (Gain of 50m over 0.1miles)
    This otherwise quite pretty street which features on many
    postcards is probably one of the more intimidating hills out of
    the Grassmarket. The combination of cobbles and impatient
    cars make this steep climb up to the castle a struggle but the
    high likelihood of someone giving a bit of a push on this
    particular knocks it down a place from Blackfriars in terms of
    difficulty.

7. Candlemaker Row (Gain of 40m over 0.2 miles)
    This hill is steep but manageable and often preferable to
    Victoria Street as although the gradient is similar the road
    surface is smooth and the gradient varies allowing you to "take
    it easy" (relatively speaking) part way up.

8. Westport (Gain of 45m over 0.2 miles)
    This hill is tough but traffic lights en-route allow you to take a
    breather (provided you are strong enough to pull away again).
    Also most lifts headed in this direction tend to be big earners
    so the psychological element is slightly easier.

9. Guthrie Street (Gain of 35m over 0.1 miles)
    Arguably tougher than Westport on a physical level but it is the
    easiest and quickest way out of the Cowgate onto the bridges
    and it is all downhill from Chambers Street to New Town. This

makes it psychologically easier than other options but many new riders have been defeated by this climb.

10. Lothian Road (Gain of 45m over 0.4 miles)
    Lothian road is fairly shallow as hills in Edinburgh go but it is a long climb with three passengers, especially in a headwind. By comparison North Bridge from the east end of Princes Street is marginally easier but both present the challenge of dealing with fast moving traffic and strong headwinds.

A Seasonal Trade?

People are often surprised that pedicabs operate all year and in all weathers as most folk seem to only encounter them during the fringe festival or at New Years Eve. This chapter will hopefully give you an insight into how things change throughout the year.

January

This is the one month most Edinburgh rickshaw drivers either dread or enjoy. For those looking to keep working it is a time of slim pickings and the most awful weather this fine city can throw at you. For others it is a chance to take time off after working the Hogmanay New Year's eve celebrations which is usually one of the most profitable nights of the year.

Given the adverse conditions and lack of customers after the Christmas spending spree there is something satisfying about still managing to earn a profit in January. You have to work hard for it but you feel like a champion on the way home, especially when it starts snowing as for Leo and Thomas below.

The Rugby

The Six Nations and Autumn Rugby Internationals at Murrayfield are events every pedicabber has marked in their diary. The reason for this is that if you are fit enough to withstand almost 40 hours of cycling within a 48 hour period then you can make several hundred pounds with some riders making in excess of £1000. During the game it is often worth trying to ply for trade however most choose to find a suitable bolt hole and watch the game. This makes it a highly sociable event to work and often causes discussions about who we want to win versus who would be better to win in terms of potential earnings. Usually this means either the Irish or the English as we know that the Scots will be out drinking regardless.

The Highland Show

The farming community of Scotland and Northern England descends upon Edinburgh each spring for a week of everything Rural, culminating in a raucous weekend out in the big city. Rickshaw drivers have a love hate relationship with this particular weekend. You can earn megabucks and most of the people are lovely. But there will also be plenty of massive blokes wanting a lift to the less desirable parts of town after they've given up trying to use their charm to attract the attention of the opposite sex.

One pedicabbers recounted his most memorable lift as:

"Taking three enormous farmers to the 'Executive Sauna' who went from being a boisterous nightmare to petrified as soon as I got them onto the dark back street upon which their desired destination was located, quite where they thought I'd take them to is a mystery....."

I'm here for the #fringe don't you know....

For centuries citizens of Edinburgh lived in fear of invasion from 'the dreaded English', in recent times though it seems that such an invasion is actively encouraged every August during the Edinburgh Fringe, Comedy and International Festival.

For three weeks each year, Edinburgh's population swells massively as it is flooded with thespians, street performers, comedians, interpretive dancers, living statues of Yoda and those wishing to watch them. Some of these acts are fantastic; others are, frankly not worth the free ticket you were given by the PR guy...

At this time of year you are more likely to hear a London or American accent than a Scottish one. For the motivated pedicabber this is big money time as you will find business at all times of day and night with theatre goers and thespians out in the daytime and partygoers hitting the clubs till 5am.

Some rickshaw driver's love this time of year with the (usually) warm weather, potential to earn big bucks and often pleasant clientele; other's however dislike the long hours, overzealous stewards and PR folk burying your cab in flyers.

Still if you are prepared to work hard and give up your social life for three weeks you can earn several thousand pounds over the course of the festival. Some riders have used this to fund trips around the world, buy a small yacht, clear debts and start successful businesses.

The Tattoo

Most of the year for some reason, slightly older members of society tend not to summon the services of pedicabs. As such at no other time will a pedicabber escort so many customers living through their golden years than in the wake of the Edinburgh Military Tattoo.

For 22 nights each August the Castle hosts one of the most spectacular shows of the Edinburgh Festival featuring marching bands, multinational dance troupes, daredevil stunts and huge fireworks. Each night after the end of the Tattoo over 4000 people spill out of the castle and proceed like a wave down the Lawnmarket.

After a few hours sat in an open air stadium many among this crowd are usually keen to get back to their hotel or coach as soon as possible and given Edinburgh's hilly terrain this is not easy for those with mobility issues.

As such there is often competition among pedicabbers for the best spot as whoever is first in the rank is likely to attract considerable business in the hour immediately after the tattoo and it is often a race against the clock to get back to the Royal Mile after completing a fare.

There are also not many sights funnier than a pair of Octogenarian ladies in the back of a rickshaw whizzing down the mound at 30mph+ as some of the pedicabbers fail to appreciate that it has probably been a while since their customers ventured onto a rollercoaster. Still the majority of customers love this bit of the lift and certainly get home faster than if they'd waited for a cab.

Halloween

Halloween is generally regarded as one of the most enjoyable and profitable nights of the year. It brings out all sorts of ghosts and ghouls onto the streets; including people who wouldn't be out on a normal Friday or Saturday night so it's guaranteed to be busy. If you want to, it is also an excellent opportunity to dress up. One rider once dressed in a 'Borat thong' but I'll save you that photo.

It's Christmas!

Christmas is a fun time of year to be a rickshaw driver in Edinburgh, generally people are in a good mood and people who wouldn't necessarily be out late the rest of the year are also out celebrating and happy to splash out on a rickshaw. It can pay off to dress up or decorate your bike and knowing the kick out times of different venues is also key to doing well in December.

That said it also seems to be the time of year with the most fights and arguments on the streets as office tensions bubble to the surface after a few too many drinks at the Christmas party. There is something comical about a bloke in a flashing Rudolph jumper scuffling with another guy in a santa suit.

New Year Generosity "Fuck it, it's only Money"

Pedicabbing is not the most consistent way to make a living; expected earnings vary seasonally and with the weather. Very, very, occasionally legend comes true and riders stumble upon people who are, for want of a better word, loaded! This can rescue a night and these people range from the discrete to the outright flamboyant. One particularly generous customer on New Year's Eve paid £100 to the rider for a relatively short fare, many times the quoted price. Upon thanking the customer for his generosity the man replied "Fuck it, it's only money, we'd planned to spunk it all tonight anyway". Although sometimes this is motivated by a desire to show off the cash, more often these guys have been in similar jobs before and now they are successful they want to help someone else along the way.

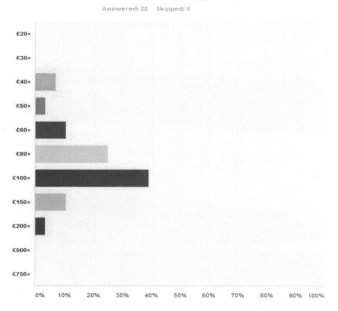

Most ever earned from a single fare?

Answered: 28   Skipped: 0

74

Rickshaw FAQ's

What Each!!!???

Understandably it is hard work negotiating Edinburgh's hilly cobbled streets with passengers in the back so the majority of riders employ a price per person policy which varies depending upon how many people are in the bike and the destination they want. It is also something of a VIP service as pedicabs can stop along the way to pick up food, take special car free routes so people can see another part of the city and drop them literally inches from their door. With certain people though the news that the price is per person can result in the shrill response of:

"What, Each?!?!?!?!", as if they've not been paying that all night for drinks.

Sometimes you know it's coming. There it goes, brows raised, eyes widen and out comes that most dreaded response. You wince in discomfort as the sound wave hits your ear-drum and the smell of kebab and beer travels on the wave of outrage.

For drivers who are highly skilled in conflict resolution the situation may be salvageable. 'I'll tell you what: if you don't think it's worth it at the end, by all means knock a few quid off'. Sometimes this can make them reconsider but usually the damage is done. Once they've uttered that single, strained syllable the chances are they're walking away. Then to add insult to injury they take great pride in pointing out that 'It'd be cheaper in a bloody taxi!' Yes. Yes it damn well would.

Top 5 Improbable Destinations:

A common heckle is to ask for somewhere really far away, precluded by the phase: "I'll give ye a fiver if ye take me te..." The top five most common of such destinations include:

1. Glasgow!
2. Manchester!
3. Fife/Dunfermline!
4. The Airport/Livingston
5. Dublin

These destinations are asked for so many times that you are unlikely even to get a reaction if you shout any of them in the direction of a rickshaw driver.

Malcolm showing off his new pricing system.

Do you get folk who don't pay?

Sometimes, but not very often. Often people won't get in if they don't want to pay but even those who think they can just run away usually pay something as they can see you've worked hard. It depends on your ability to turn a situation around in your favour.

An example of people who don't pay.

Pedicabbers claim to have a sense for when someone might be trouble but some folk slip right under the radar. It is just the worst when your chatty and apparently very friendly customer suddenly goes quiet with the only trace of him or her being the sound of flat feet smacking off the pavement as they peg it down an alley. There is very little you can do in this situation unless a police car happens to be passing and he's elected to leg it down a dead end. If however your customer tries this when you drop them off at a nightclub you can always tell the bouncer who 9/10 times will not let them in.

The Shawbusters' Personal Tales

This section gets up close and personal with a few of the rickshaw drivers/riders whatever you wish to call them and those who run the companies which rent them out to riders. All are people with whom the author of this book has worked. Everyone was asked the same four basic questions:

Some riders had lengthy stories to tell and happily provided a key insight into the history of rickshaws in Edinburgh that many people aren't aware of. There's also a great deal of humour in there too.

Laura Margaret Baird

Age: *32*

Time on the 'shaws: *One Year, since June 2015*

Why Rickshaws?
I originally wanted to start rickshawing to spend more time with my other half; he was shawbusting almost every weekend at the time and you'd be guaranteed to see his smile on a shift.

It was a challenge, mentally and physically for me. But after getting shadowed a few weekends in a row I got in the groove of Edinburgh and relaxed into it nicely. There was also something appealing about challenging myself to do as well as the boys because the Edinburgh Rickshaw scene is quite male dominated. In doing so I'd be proving to myself and other women you can do anything as long as you set your mind to it.

What do you do outside of rickshawing and what are your future plans?

Rickshawing allowed me to rethink my career in childcare and pursue what makes me happy. Being active and happy and meeting new people everyday made the change happen. I now work in retail in a small independent business and I'm looking to go in jewellery make course at uni in the new year. Rickshawing has encouraged me to become more committed to my own goals.

What is your most memorable fare?

The most memorable fare I have had? It's a tough question, I've had customers who have made me laugh so much I've had to pull over to control my belly laugh then there's customers who have hired me for the night to take them on pub crawls, I think my most strange one was a celeb I picked up on George street to save from a mass of crowded women screaming, I sang him one of his songs "I'm flying without wings" as I rang the bell cycling by him!! He jumped in thanked me for saving him, then ran out at next cash machine and never paid!!!!

Willie's Story

By choice or otherwise, Edinburgh has a large number of homeless people. Current government austerity policies have made the situation worse, forcing many people onto the streets. Among them are also a number of "professional beggars" who turn up in normal clothes before putting on a scruffy jacket to beg for a couple of hours. As Pedicab drivers we see who the 'real' homeless are and get to know a few of the characters, many of these people also have some of the best trained dogs I've ever seen. You'll often see a dog holding a hat in its mouth for passersby to put change in. Willie and his dog Toby got to know the pedicab drivers and then went on to hit the streets as a pedicab driver and get himself back on track. He now rarely rickshaws as he's found other work which he prefers.

Leo Bruges

"Described by some as the Jedi master of rickshawing".

Age: 36

Time on the rickshaws to date: 16 years (Since august 2000)

Leo was among the original rickshaw drivers in Edinburgh. As he says *"It all started with Phil Varley who moved here from San Francisco and set up Edinburgh pedicabs in 1999. When he began recruiting new riders in the summer of 2000 I decided to give it a go. In the beginning demand for bikes often meant riders had to wait but thanks to Phil being good at teaching others the best sales method for the job earnings were good so the fleet grew. You could say that Phil's methods are still being used today".*

Why Rickshaws?

"I've never had the patience for an office job. I've done all sorts, care work, dishwashing you name it but they are all relatively low paid. I discovered that Rickshaws allowed me to work outside and make good money fast. The

combination of challenge for mind and body along with sociability is also attractive. I'm a natural introvert but when rickshawing my character changes allowing an extrovert side of me to come out which is really fun! It is also a handy way to help support my family, I have a partner and two children so this allows me to top up my income from being a film maker"

How has rickshawing changed since the early days?

"It wasn't always about fitness; the best drivers were not necessarily the fittest. It was more about personality and fun, as it still is. The old guard as I call them were certainly not as fit as the new riders. It used to be common for the riders to stay up after work and have a piss up for several hours till late morning after finishing work at 4am.

The new guard are probably the fittest crop of Edinburgh rickshaw drivers ever to hit the streets. More than half are seriously into their cycling with a couple of semi-professional cyclists and numerous serious amateurs within the ranks. Leggings and lycra only appeared about three years ago but now most riders are pretty sporty which is a big change from the old guard. By that I mean they are still really keen on socialising with other riders but it is less about booze and more about other activities. You'll often see riders disappear off quickly after work so they can get a few hours sleep before a big race."

What is your most memorable fare?

"There are so many... Of recent memory it was august (2015) when I was sat at the top of Victoria street. A guy in tattoos and a tee approached me and offered me a hundred quid Leith walk. He had a heavy metal hairdo and had a guy and a girl with him. The main thing I remember is that his friends didn't seem to mind him acting like a bit of a dick so long as he kept flashing the cash. Like when we stopped at a pie shop he thought it was funny to throw pie in the girl's face and they all laughed but it seemed a bit forced. In the end he gave me a decent tip turning it into probably my biggest fare ever. I never would have asked for what he gave me but that's what he thought it was worth. It's fairly common for people to show off in this way, paying well above what anyone would have quoted for the fare. It is usually out of a feeling that they want to pay their fortune forward or some kind of insecurity.

Either way it's nice when these rare lifts come along as the average fare for most lifts is £15-£20 and we certainly work hard for that. Often I find a hug or a handshake more rewarding than a tip (I mean both are nice) as at least you know it has been a good interaction. In some ways I see the big lifts as cheating in this game about making money and a living but I'm pretty sure I'll spend it better than they will."

"I also have a couple of others that stick in the memory, a Japanese guy once gave me £100 to go from CC blooms to his hotel. He didn't really speak much English but I think he might have thought he was buying me too... The other one is representative of a lot of people out on the town who find themselves doing some soul searching. He'd taken ecstasy for the first time in his life and wanted sex. There are places in Edinburgh where he could go for this and usually I'd have no problem taking someone there as it's not my place to judge where people want to go. On this occasion though he wanted some advice, he needed to discuss it with someone. That someone happened to be me. He'd been in a relationship with a woman he loved for over eight years but felt like he needed a night to let go, be irresponsible for once. We discussed all this during the fare and when we arrived I tried to dissuade him from going in but in the end he still decided to do so."

What's the most important thing for a fare?

"Number one: to get paid, number two that the customers enjoy it and three be very clear and upfront about pricing. This means that 90% of the time you don't get into trouble as everyone knows what they are getting at the beginning of the fare".

How do you deal with those that still cause trouble or refuse to pay?

"It's usually about reminding them of the verbal contract you had. If they didn't want to pay the price quoted they shouldn't have got in. Just as I cannot suddenly double the fare, the passenger should not be able to get away without paying as that is effectively theft. Some people are thrillseekers, they are out on the town to escape. With these people you need to bring them

down to earth for a second and remind them that this is your livelihood and that you have a family depending on you.

If that fails I try embarrassing them in front of their friends, saying they can't afford it but sometimes you just have to cut your losses. You make the calculation that standing there arguing when you could get another fare will probably cost you more money or you are only a couple of quid short and some meat heads want an excuse to start a fight. To last you certainly need to be mentally resilient, capable of forgiveness (quickly) and let the negativity of the 10% or so of bad customers wash off you like water off a ducks back. If you are ever unsure always ask for the money upfront, if they don't pay then it is fine to let them walk away rather than waste your energy on them by risking them not paying at the end of the fare.

I've known some riders lose out after being promised hundreds of pounds for really long journeys only to return empty handed or worse... In the end it's a battle of egos you have to give off the air of being a nice guy but don't fuck with me. Local knowledge also helps with security as you know where to bolt to if you need to and being on the bike seems to give you some kind of invisible forcefield allowing you to glide through situations which may otherwise be dangerous.

Always Always *keep money in a safe place, never in a place passengers can reach. I once had some guys steal from me without realising who were cheeky enough to pay me with my own money at the end of the fare."*

What do you do outside of rickshawing?

"I'm a filmmaker, I make documentaries mainly but also do freelance camera work. Ten years ago I won a BAFTA new talent award for a fist full of roses inspired by a guy called Innis Wood who used to sell flowers around Edinburgh at night but felt he had to wear a stab vest. It was filmed over four nights in a six month period and made into a 30 minute and a o minute documentary. My long term aim is to make a living out of filmmaking but I've not managed to yet as I don't want to do anything commercial. Also supporting my family is a priority and I hope to complete a Masters in Cinematography in London at some point as this would be a big step toward leaving rickshawing behind. I've threatened to quit a few times but it allows me time with family and to pursue my other interests so for now I'm sticking with it."

Matthew Jackson

Age: *25*

Time on the rickshaws to date: *4 years* (Started October 2013)

Why Rickshaws?

"Initially it was due to a love of cycling, now however money is a more major motivator for me. It also gives me a lot of free time to do what I want to do such as train for actual cycle races. Last year I won the Edinburgh road club time trial league, Arthur's seat hill climb, unofficial fixed gear TT championship and WISE BMC bike messenger championships. This year I'm planning on winning several more titles however. A standard full time job it would make it impossible for me to train effectively for this. "

What is your most memorable fare?

"A couple of years ago during fresher's week, one lift involved going up Guthrie Street with three quite large people in the back. Seemingly out of

nowhere a massive crowd of students appeared and lined the street cheering me on the whole way up. I also hold the record for most people transported by aid of a single rickshaw to the strippers. A 32 strong stag do paid me once to cycle the stag and the best man on the condition that I went very slowly so that they could follow on foot and laugh at him the whole way."

In the future?

"My current plan is to set up a media and advertising business using Adbikes and leaflet distribution in Edinburgh (Thunderdome Media). I will be participating in a number of national cycle racing championships.

In the near future I also hope to break the Scottish hour record for longest distance cycled within 60 minutes (Currently 46.65km or 187 laps of a velodrome). It has been held for nearly 20 years with no attempts made on it in that time. If I've done enough training I would like to achieve this at the Meadowbank velodrome in Edinburgh as this is where the record was previously set and it is likely to be demolished soon as the council want to re-develop the site."

Ben Simpson (The Doctor)

Age: 31

Time on the Rickshaws to date:

4 years (Started July 2012)

Why Rickshaws?

"Frankly I started because of my awful finances after my graduate medical degree and my younger brother suggested it. I also had a small daughter and my wife was unable to work. Throughout my medical training rickshawing was my main income. Although now I'm working full time as a doctor it helps top up earnings. Believe it or not but doctors don't actually get paid much these days... over the years I've managed to earn more from rickshawing than my main job. It has allowed me to turn my family's finances around so we are in a much more secure position now."

What is your most memorable fare?

"There aren't many that stick out, most are enjoyable but it gets a bit repetitive. Probably my favourite was when I gave the CEO of Rockstar North a lift. He was good fun and liked sharing his cash; the agreement was two rickshaws from Cowgate across town to near India Place with £100 going to whoever got there first. As we struggled up Victoria Street he got distracted and got out to talk to people while his pal helped me by pushing the bike to make sure we got to the top first but we still had to wait for him. This left us behind so (sensing a big reward) I admit to bending the road rules a little as we zoomed down the mound to catch up. At the end the group had had a brilliant time and Mr Rockstar paid us £450 each. To think I almost didn't work that weekend!"

Murray MacDonald

Age: 23

Time on the rickshaws to date: 3.5 years (Since September 2012)

Why Rickshaws?

"After I moved to Edinburgh from Oban I needed a job and wanted to make new friends. The process was fairly easy. I was invited for training after replying to the ad and once I had my license I was soon out on the streets plying for trade. I really enjoyed meeting people in the first week and value many of the other riders as close friends including my best friend Tom Nurick. This has also allowed me to become more financially independent and learn how to manage my Autism"

What is your most memorable fare?

"Probably during the Edinburgh Fringe 2013 when I gave a lift to a guy from Grassmarket to George Street. He is probably my most generous fare to date. He talked about how he'd strived to be independent from an early age and seemed impressed with my efforts to live independently and pursue the things I want to do in life without relying on my family for financial support. After the journey we shook hands and to my surprise he gave me £150 i.e. 712% of the originally agreed £20 fare!"

Outside of rickshawing and future plans?

"I'm a keen sailor; I have a few races lined up this year. I once made the mistake of taking a group of rickshawers out on a sail with me being the only one with sailing experience. It turned into a bit more of a booze cruise (on their part) than I had expected and was probably the scariest thing I have ever done as we nearly hit the harbour wall but it makes a good story now. I'm currently studying toward an access course at the University of Edinburgh as I'd like to do an English Literature or Creative Writing Degree. I'm planning to start writing books about my regular cycle tours around Scotland too. Alongside all that I've also started my own charitable foundation called 'Autism on the Water' to promote awareness of autism and provide support for people with Autism."

Genevieve Whitson

Age: 35

Time of the rickshaws to date: 2.5 years (Since May 2013)

Why Rickshaws?

"I'm an elite cyclist and needed a way to help fund my racing career. Rickshawing allows me to make money and is also brilliant training, particularly for longer races. A 3 hour race now seems much easier than an 8 hour rickshaw shift. There is also an excellent social scene and there have been some excellent nights out. For example on a Christmas drinks night out a couple of years ago, one of the guys was planning to cycle back to Dundee after the pub as he'd done it quite a few times. A few whiskies later (and a detour to my flat to get my bike and work clothes for the next day) I found

myself along with Xani, Thomas and Tim on the Forth Road Bridge at 1am on my way to Dundee. We arrived about 4am, Xani and Tim were able to stay and have a fry up while Thomas and I got the first train back to Edinburgh as we had to get to work. When I arrived at the office and went to change I realised that drunken me had managed to pack some very ridiculous clothes..."

Most memorable fare?

"As a female rider I probably get some slightly stranger requests than some of the guys. One bloke once paid me an extra fiver at the end of a fare to let him sniff my saddle...."

Future plans?

"I work in fundraising and development for the Scottish Rural University College (SRUC.) I've also just picked up a new sponsor to supply me with bikes and equipment for cycle racing. I'm not quite sure where I'll go next, it depends on what happens with cycling"

Steven Anderson

Age: 31

Time on the shaws: Just over a year (Since December 2014)

Why Rickshaws?

"I'm comfortable cycling long distances so this sounded perfect as it meant I could earn money while exercising and chatting to people. That said it took me a while to get used to it and I failed the first time I went for training with one company. I tried again with another company who gave me a bit more time to get used to the bike as the steering is really weird compared to a standard bike. At first I was out every week but now I'm not so strict and go out when I feel like it".

What is your most memorable fare?

"Probably my first night, I'd say your first night is a bit like when you've just had a haircut. When you meet people you expect them to know because you know you've had a haircut but they've only just met you so don't know any different. Yeah it's a bit like that, people ask you to go somewhere and expect

you to know where it is so it was a bit hard at first. I also didn't really know what to charge so did some silly lifts for very little money. The level of silliness did get rather high, for example I did a lift up west port to Lothian road with two big guys and only asked for a fiver at the end of it. I mean I was happy that I'd proved to myself that I could do it but did make a mental note to increase my fares a tad, partly to avoid other riders questioning my sanity for doing such a hard lift so cheaply".

Outside of rickshawing?

"I'm still working on that but I'm enjoying having some flexibility in when I work as it means I get to spend more time with my partner."

Sam Downing

Age: 21

(Aged 18 when started and proudly bore the title of youngest rickshaw driver until very recently)

Time on the shaws:

3.5 years (Since October 2012)

Why Rickshaws?

"I grew up on Mull and was seriously into bike racing throughout my teens. After moving to Edinburgh to study at Herriot Watt I managed to blow £2000 in freshers' week so had to find some way to earn that money back. I mean I don't remember much of that week but it must have been excellent. A friend of mine suggested rickshawing and given that I was a strong cyclist and wanted to get to know the city a bit more. It was my first time in the big city and the income gave me a chance to be independent. I had to grow up quickly but most of the other riders still think of me as the baby of the pedicab world"

What is your most memorable fare?

"There are a few but probably the time I took this guy who wanted to go to the Holiday Inn on the Cowgate. When he got in he gave me a big wodge of cash, I tried to give some back as it wasn't that far but he insisted. After a few minutes we got there and as the guy was walking to enter the hotel I thought I'd make a silly joke and asked for a tip. His response was hilarious, there he was stood in the doorway rummaging through his pockets and throwing whatever coins and notes he could at me while shouting "You cheeky Fuck! You know how much I gave you! Here's some more fucking change for your brass balls!" With a cheeky wink he then continued into his hotel while I went around picking up all the money he'd thrown in my general direction."

Outside of Rickshawing

"I decided to quit Uni after first year as I wasn't enjoying my Maths degree and wanted to train as a plumber. To fund this I started working seven days a week, alongside rickshawing I used to work as a cycle courier and mechanic for B-Spokes which used to be the biggest rickshaw company in Edinburgh. I also worked for a Mexican restaurant and a few other odd jobs. I must've clocked up a few hundred hour weeks but it paid off as I managed to save up quite a bit. Probably the hardest week was summer 2014 during the fringe when I woke up at 8am to get to my Courier job delivering parcels by cargo bike until 5pm then worked 6pm till 10pm delivering food for the restaurant. I did this all week until Friday when I then went straight from deliveries to working on the rickshaw until 6am. After a couple of hours sleep I was then back on deliveries until 9pm (with a lot of coffee and the odd cat nap). At 10pm I then went back out on the bikes till the early hours. This went on for another two weeks until the end of the festival. I enjoyed the challenge and am proud that I managed it but it did make me a bit grumpy..."

I'm now back at Heriot Watt but as staff doing an engineering apprenticeship and college course. After working so much I'm enjoying having more of a standard work week with free time. I'm essentially retired from rickshawing but may do an odd shift every now and then."

Ross Jenkins

Age: 33

Time on the shaws: *2.5 years (since 2013) but recently had a six month break due to a recurring knee injury.*

Why Rickshawing?

I'm an entrepreneur keen to help others in society. Rickshawing allowed me to work the weekend and devote the rest of the week to setting up a social enterprise (among other businesses) to help homeless people transition from homelessness to tenancy. This enables them to get back into work or at least secure housing benefit and get off the street. The idea is to provide accommodation, food and work experience in exchange for labour in the form of on the job training. It is this which allows me to create an income stream which is fed back into the business. The aim is to provide a missing stepping stone for those who have recently been homeless but need help managing things in the first few months of a tenancy as this is when most end up back on the streets due to a lack of other support available. I also design websites and sell bamboo toothbrushes.

What is your most memorable fare?

"I don't like the festival particularly but during the first one I worked I had one really enjoyable lift that sticks out. I had been sat outside the castle for over an hour and was starting to get disheartened about the prospects of getting a fare.

Then just before I was about to give up A fellow rider (Amadeusz Gorski) secured a fare requiring two rickshaws, at first it seemed like they were two elderly couples but I later learned they were members of a bus tour that had come to Edinburgh and had some time to kill. It started as a quick tour of the old town around some of the key sights and ending in the Grassmarket for £25 per bike.

At the Grassmarket there were some buskers and Don and Faye were really enjoying just sitting in the bike watching the world around them while I was able to give them a bit more of a local understanding of what they were seeing. They had also enjoyed the excitement of the downhill sections.

After a few minutes they asked to extend the tour so we agreed a half hourly rate and I suggested we start with the new town and work from there. After going around George Street and onto St Andrews Square they asked where the best place to get a decent view of Edinburgh and the surrounding area.

I figured Arthur's Seat wouldn't be accessible by rickshaw so we agreed on Calton Hill, it was tough but I made it up to the top. Once there we stopped for a bit, Don (who turned out to be a man of the cloth) got out of the bike to buy us all coffee and ice cream.

About half an hour went past with them pointing to things asking what they were such as Murrayfield Stadium and the Parliament; they then asked if they could have a closer look at Holyrood Palace. Don and Faye really enjoyed the ride there as it was all downhill along regent road.

A few minutes after we arrived they noticed the time and realised they soon had to meet the rest of the coach party for dinner which meant I had to take them all the way back up to the castle. Ordinarily this would be daunting but I had enjoyed the lift so much so far that I felt like I had the energy for it.

The middle section of the Royal Mile (High Street) was closed so I had to take a long detour via St Mary's street then Cowgate and up Candlemaker Row.

Various passersby were kind enough to help along some of the steeper sections before finally making it up to George IV bridge and the top of the Royal Mile. Somehow we managed to make it earlier than I'd expected so offered to cycle them around some more but Don insisted that I treat the money for that extra time as my tip.

Don also gave me his email address and later informed me that the tour I gave them was the highlight of their holiday. After they went into the restaurant I decided to go home on a good note as thanks to them I'd more than exceeded my target for the day and had a lovely few hours.

Oskar Kudłacz Górski

Age: 22

Time on the Shaws: *Around one and a half years, December 2014 to July 2016*

Why Rickshawing?

Rickshawing because there were fun people, good money, flexible hours and I could skip a leg day in the gym from time to time

What is your most memorable fare?

Unfortunately my most memorable moment was when I was doing a double lift down Cowgate with another rickshaw driver and the police stopped us because they thought we were racing. We were cycling next to each other but weren't exactly racing. The whole thing ended up in court. We had to make three appearances in court, during the last one everything was supposed to be resolved but the policemen who were the only witnesses for the prosecution did not show up. So luckily they let us go with no ticket to pay.

Outside of Rickshawing:

I recently moved to Poland where I grew up to do a 12 month placement for my 3rd year. I do plan to move back to Edinburgh though so hopefully I'll be back on the shaw' for a little while yet.

Quincy

Age: 27

Time of the Shaws:

"Circa two years on and off since the week before Wimbledon Tennis Championships of 2014"

Why Rickshaws?

"In short it is great exercise, keeps me from drinking at the weekends while still having fun and earning decent dollar. I work most weekends and go by the pseudonym Quincy. He's my rickshawing alter ego as when I work I find that I morph into a different character."

What is your most memorable fare?

"In the early days of my venture into rickshawing I was struggling up the Mound with some ladies in the back. They were good fun, singing we will rock you the whole way. About a third of the way up a bit group of lads decided to help out by forming a scrimmage behind me and pushing me the rest of the way up. When we got to the top we all stopped to dance and sing together before parting ways."

Outside of rickshawing?

"I like to make music and I'm studying Economics at PhD level. In the long run I'd like to set up and run a small events business with an ethical slant. I'm hoping to stay healthy and active while working to realise some worthy ideals of mine".

Robbie Aitkien

Age: 24

Time on the rickshaws: 3 Years since May 2013

Why Rickshaws?

"At first, because I was jobless after getting fed up with Mcdonalds but I stuck with it because the money is good and the girls are good. What I mean by that is that It's a good way to meet people; an instant talking point so to speak. I also like that each night is different. You have to be prepared to put yourself out there and see what happens."

What is your most memorable fare?

"During the festival soon after I started I gave a lift to three girls who were doing comedy. I ended up meeting up with them again later on and I'm still in contact with them. One of them is now in Hollyoaks, it's nice making new friends and seeing them become more successful. The other one which springs to mind was when three American guys gave me triple the fare from Haymarket to George street just for being a good story teller, it's when you meet folk like that which makes you feel good about what you're doing"

Outside of Pedicabbing?

"I'm a support worker but looking to join the navy. Rickshawing has funded a lot of adventures but I now want something more substantial. It's been a good ride so I may as well quit while I'm ahead."

Nikolay Trifonou

Age: 30

Time on the 'shaws: *"5 years, I started in 2011"*

Why Rickshawing?

"I like to take my time with things. Before starting as a rickshaw driver I'd been living in Edinburgh for four years after moving from Bulgaria. It looked like fun so I'd wanted to give it a go for a while and I'd been a passenger a few times too just to see what it was like.I like the social scene and the up for anything attitude of many of the other riders. Once after a shift we went for a swim down at Portobello beach, it was f###in' freezing!"

What is your most memorable fare?

"I used to regularly work the Thursday nights to try to cover the weekend's rent for the bike. It's usually pretty quiet midweek so I never expected to earn as much as a weekend night.   Once at around 10pm I was sat on the Grassmarket when two guys came up to me wanting to go to the airport. I was up for the challenge and quoted them £150 as it is a considerable distance. They manage to haggle me down to £50 as it was really quiet and I needed the money. After whizzing down the Grassmarket and along past Lothian road they decided to take a taxi the rest of the way so I helped them flag one down. I offered to give them back some of the fare but they said to keep it which was very kind of them. I was also relieved! I mean I was crapping myself about having to cycle all that way, it's about 10 miles!"

Anonymous Recounts of Riders favourite or most memorable fares:

"I had a couple in the back who hadn't seen each other for a while. She kept wanting to give him a BJ in the back but he was insisting she wait until they got back to the hotel. As I was cycling round Charlotte square about a minute from the hotel when I heard her say come on just the tip. After things went quiet I turned round and saw her face in his lap moving up and down underneath the blanket. He shouted way hay and reached up to high five me. I didn't leave him hanging. Seemed rude not to. Classy people."

"You often get really nice customers, it's a shame the idiots tend to stick in the mind more readily. I like nice customers as it really gives me a boost particularly on nights where I'm lacking any kind of inner drive".

"Too many to count. Any time going downhill fast. Especially Cockburn Street. The 80 pound lift was from Grassmarket to Cav/Lava - guy agreed on 30 and then gave me a 50 pound tip. Or asking a gorgeous Italian girl if she wanted a lift and her responding 'no I want you.' This led to 1 hour making out in the back of the rickshaw. But probably an afternoon summer lift with a mum and

two kids from the castle to Bruntsfield through the Meadows was my favourite. Went on the grass and everything. Delightful."

"The chicken handjob: I once had a girl start stroking my face with a raw chicken breast. When I complained, she then shoved it down my shorts while I was riding and attempted to start giving me a handjob with the piece of chicken. Then when I also complained about this she apologised and proceeded to start eating the raw chicken."

"This one group I picked up from the Caves after a wedding reception consisted of two guys and a girl. It was clear they'd been discussing the possibility of a threesome during the evening as the woman was being pretty friendly with both of them and was actively pushing a discussion about how it would work. That was until outside the kebab shop, while one of the guys was inside she found out that the other one was married. Turned out the other two were still up for it but were disappointed he hadn't been honest. The rest of the journey then consisted of the married guy having a moral debate with himself while the other two with a seemingly sincere opinion that it was down to what he felt was right were acting as angel on the one side and agent provocateur on the other. They were still discussing it as I left them at the premier inn but it was an interesting insight into the battle between the conflicting desires many people have."

"Well this one time the rider I was on a group lift with, stud that he is, managed to pull a gaggle of hens. We took two bike loads to their hotel and my word they took a shine to him. He was reluctant but always a man for adventure was keen. I promised not to mention him locking his bike - well hidden anyway - and I left him to it. Quite a tale he had to tell later. Legend."

"The night 3 guys in the grassmarket told me they wouldn't get in my rickshaw unless I took my shorts off and rode up the grassmarket with the 3 of them in the rickshaw, while I stood out of the saddle so they could perve at my arse (I did have lyrca on!). I was prepared to do it because they paid me well and I didn't get my arse touched."

"I tore a wheel off one of Griegs bike's in an emergency stop downhill on west port. Looked up to see my wee sister (who lived far away at the time) of all *people standing about 2 feet away. I called Grieg, he brought me a new bike and I got to see him walk his busted bike up Candlemaker Row on 2 wheels. Also flying down Broughton Street in torrential downpour singing Maroon 5 with passengers and all loving it."*

"I once got paid with an E and a porno, which is a good night in!"

"You'd have to have been there"

"The time a female passenger had a mini orgasm due to the vibrations from whizzing down a cobbled street"

"A lift down to Easter Rd when the guy jumped off and I tried to chase him so I went even further down towards the Leith Links and then he disappeared in a dark alley, on the way back I took two guys from Queen street to George Street and at the top of George St. they jumped off and ran away. So that was the greatest loss I ever made."

"About 6 18 year olds tried to mug me near Studio 24 in front of a bunch of their lady friends during the festival. I'd been on a blinder and was super pumped up. Refused to hand anything over, when one of them approached me to try and fight I bitch slapped him, he started crying at the shock and the rest ran away."

"Telling 3 Norweigens it was £20 from Grassmarket to George Street, they said ok. When we got there, they got out and gave me £20 each and just wandered off. Crazy Scandinavians."

"Probably the time I was kissed by a stunning Irish chick outside her hotel while she sent her boyfriend up to the room to "get a camera so we can get a photo". Also I carried Amy Macdonald and the fat bird from Gossip around in my cab at Connect Festival in 2009. All in all though just the camaraderie of the early days of working; the money was crazy good (if you worked hard) and everyone would stay behind and drink beers. It was like a family. Totally awesome!"

"Some passengers were giving me some grief on one lift and when one of them tried to compensate for this by saying "I couldn't do this it looks really hard" unfortunately my mental filter wasn't working so when I thought to myself "I bet you couldn't you fat bitch" I actually said it out loud. Her so called friends thought this was quite funny and ended up tipping me extra."

"Mostly involving happy customers and busy nights but I struggle to remember any specific ones. Interestingly I remember all the fights quite clearly (I'd better as I'm going to court as a witness soon!)."

"Getting chased on the Pedicab while carrying pizza under my arm going up from the Holyrood Parliament after a snogging a customer who decided to kiss me and give me pizza as a tip, not realising she had a boyfriend and that he was watching from the window. Probably the funniest bit about that story was that after shouting down from their top floor flat in a Dumbiebykes tower block he ran down the stairs and you could see him zigzagging his way down through the glass. I probably should have left more time to cycle away rather than watch this though..."

"Too many to choose. It's actually pretty fun on occasion"

"I took two prostitutes to a client. They had a slut app on their phone and the pimp call centre set them up with the punter. They also showed me their minge... I have a photo, but I guess you won't use it in the book anyway."

"Gave a lift to a girl who had some really messed up mind. Her mood changed from being sad to being terrified that her father will see her on a rickshaw, then she thought I was her boyfriend and after I refused to kiss her (believe me that was a right decision) she got furious and quite violent where she tried breaking my bike etc. In the end she stole my blanket and ran away. Anyway either her mind was really messed up or she was tripping quite badly :D"

"The time I was given two sacks full of pastries and three loaves of bread by two drunk passengers who turned out to be from one of the polish bakers. This was on top of the cash fare."

"When clients invited me for a beer after my last lift. It was delicious."

"Hard to say. Every weekend there is a new story, and old ones are forgotten. One time though. I did give Danny Macaskill a lift home with a few of his mates, then (as it was the last lift of the night) dropped the bike off at the garage and went to a house party with him and a load of other hardcore partiers. A couple of other pedicabbers came too, and we hit up this house party in our sweaty rickshaw gear. Inside, Danny was attempting to bunnyhop

up an entire flight of stairs on this old piece of shit bike that he had found in the stairwell. Despite how absolutely sloshed he was, he still managed to make it up the stairs without 1) touching the walls and 2) putting his feet on the ground. Incredible tekkers (I even have a video somewhere). Then, after much anticipation, he climbed on to the shoulders of some guy, who then sat on the bike and launched himself (and Danny) back down the stairs. This was not as skilfully carried out as the ascent, and both guys came crashing off the bike mid staircase and tumbled down the stairs together, followed by the bike. The funny thing was that when Danny got up and took his t-shirt off (to inspect the damage I guess?!) his shoulder blade was almost poking through his skin. I told him that he should probably get that checked out but he looked down, looked up, shrugged his shoulders and said "naw, that always happens..."

"Being offered a part in a passenger's next porno. You never know who you're going to meet or what you might see."

"Two youngish guys asked me how much to the Travel Lodge at the Shore. I gave them a price and then they said "how much if we're naked?", "same price" I say. They then jump in and off we get. They strip off in the cab and expose themselves to passersby, get out at traffic lights to get in a taxi full of girls (who scream and chuck them out), many passersby shout in disgust/encouragement as we head down Leith walk. By the time we're on Pilrig Street the passersby are few and far between, but they're still naked and still laughing. They kept asking passers the time while posed full frontal so that when they turned around to answer they'd get a horrific eyeful. We eventually get there, they tip well and I trudge off feeling amused but denigrated."

"Getting trapped between two sets of bollards in front of the US Embassy, making quite a lot of noise trying to get out and constantly worrying I would be arrested by scary men in suits"

"A Girl dropping her pizza in a pool of sick, then picking up said pizza and continuing her feast"

"I once did a lift from the Cowgate to Captain's bar, quite a short lift but a fierce climb to I quoted them £8 each i.e. £16 total. The guy pushed for a bit too which was nice. I think he was trying to impress the woman who elected to stay in the cab. At the end of the fare despite his efforts she insisted he tip me so he simply said to keep the change from the £20 note which I was happy with. She then kept demanding he give me more saying "Give him another one!" By the time she was satisfied that I had been properly paid he'd handed over £60. She wandered into the pub singing my praises while he shook my hand and gave me a nod as if to say "I know it's not your fault but you've just taken all my money." He must've been keen to impress her to pay that much."

"At the end of a relatively innocuous fare from Grassmarket up to Frankenstein's bar on George IV Bridge I was given a £60 on one condition. I had to banish the "scary monster clown" sat on the pavement. I hadn't noticed but it now became very clear that this girl was on some kind of hallucinogenic drug. By the "scary monster clown" she simply meant the guy dressed in a luminous t-shirt sat on the opposite side of the pavement. He was nothing to do with the group but she felt threatened. I stuck around just long enough to ensure she was able to "escape" safely. When the group left I simply cycled off slightly puzzled but £70 richer. No imaginary clowns were harmed in the making of this lift".

Final Thoughts

Hopefully this has been an enjoyable recount of the world of the Rickshaw drivers in Edinburgh and encouraged you to take one every once in a while or maybe even do the training and enter the world of pedicabbing yourself.

For the author of this book it has been an enjoyable way to say goodbye as he retires from the world of rickshaws. It has been an enjoyable and highly memorable pastime however one does need to recognise when the mental and physical burden of rickshawing has become too much to juggle with other passions in life. Many thanks to those who have contributed to the making of this book as it would not have been impossible without your assistance.

Printed in Great Britain
by Amazon